IF YOU WERE A KID AT THE
MARCH ON WASHINGTON

BY JOSH GREGORY AND AARON TALLEY · ILLUSTRATED BY ANA LATESE

CHILDREN'S PRESS®

An Imprint of Scholastic Inc.

Special thanks to our consultant, Dr. Le'Trice Donaldson, assistant professor of history at Auburn University, for making sure the nonfiction text of this book is authentic and historically accurate.

NOTE TO THE READER, PARENT, LIBRARIAN, AND TEACHER: This book combines a historical fiction narrative with nonfiction fact boxes. While all the nonfiction fact boxes are historically accurate and true, the fiction comes solely from the imaginations of the authors and illustrator.

Library of Congress Cataloging-in-Publication Data available

ISBN 978-1-5461-3622-4 (library binding) / ISBN 978-1-5461-3623-1 (paperback)

10 9 8 7 6 5 4 3 2 1   25 26 27 28 29

Printed in China 62
First edition, 2025

Book design by Kathleen Petelinsek

Photos ©: 9: Dinodia Photos/Alamy Images; 11: Afro American Newspapers/Gado/Getty Images; 13: Keystone/Hulton Archive/Getty Images; 15: Morton Broffman/Getty Images; 17: Bill Preston/The Tennessean-USA TODAY NETWORK/Imagn; 19: Paul Schutzer/The LIFE Picture Collection/Shutterstock; 21: AP Photo; 23: Stocktrek Images, Inc./Alamy Images; 25: California African American Museum; 27: LBJ Library photo by Cecil Stoughton.

TABLE OF CONTENTS

A Different Way of Life

The 1960s were a time of change in the United States. For decades, **segregation** and **Jim Crow laws** had kept Black, Latino, Asian, and **Indigenous** people from enjoying the same rights and privileges as white people. Black people, for example, were often forced to live in rundown neighborhoods. Unfair laws kept them from voting or getting good jobs. Black children were not allowed to attend the same schools as white children.

By 1963, the **civil rights** movement was in full swing. Protestors from all ethnic groups and religions from across the country were fighting back against unfair treatment. They organized marches, held **sit-ins**, and used other nonviolent methods to fight for freedom and equality. One of the biggest events of the movement was the March on Washington for Jobs and Freedom, an enormous demonstration held in Washington, D.C.

Turn the page to visit this important moment in U.S. history!

Meet Eugene!

Eugene lives with his family in Washington, D.C., in a mostly Black neighborhood called Barry Farm. Quiet and polite, he doesn't like to see people fight. He knows the civil rights movement is important, and he admires the peaceful message of Dr. Martin Luther King, Jr. But does protesting have to be so dangerous?

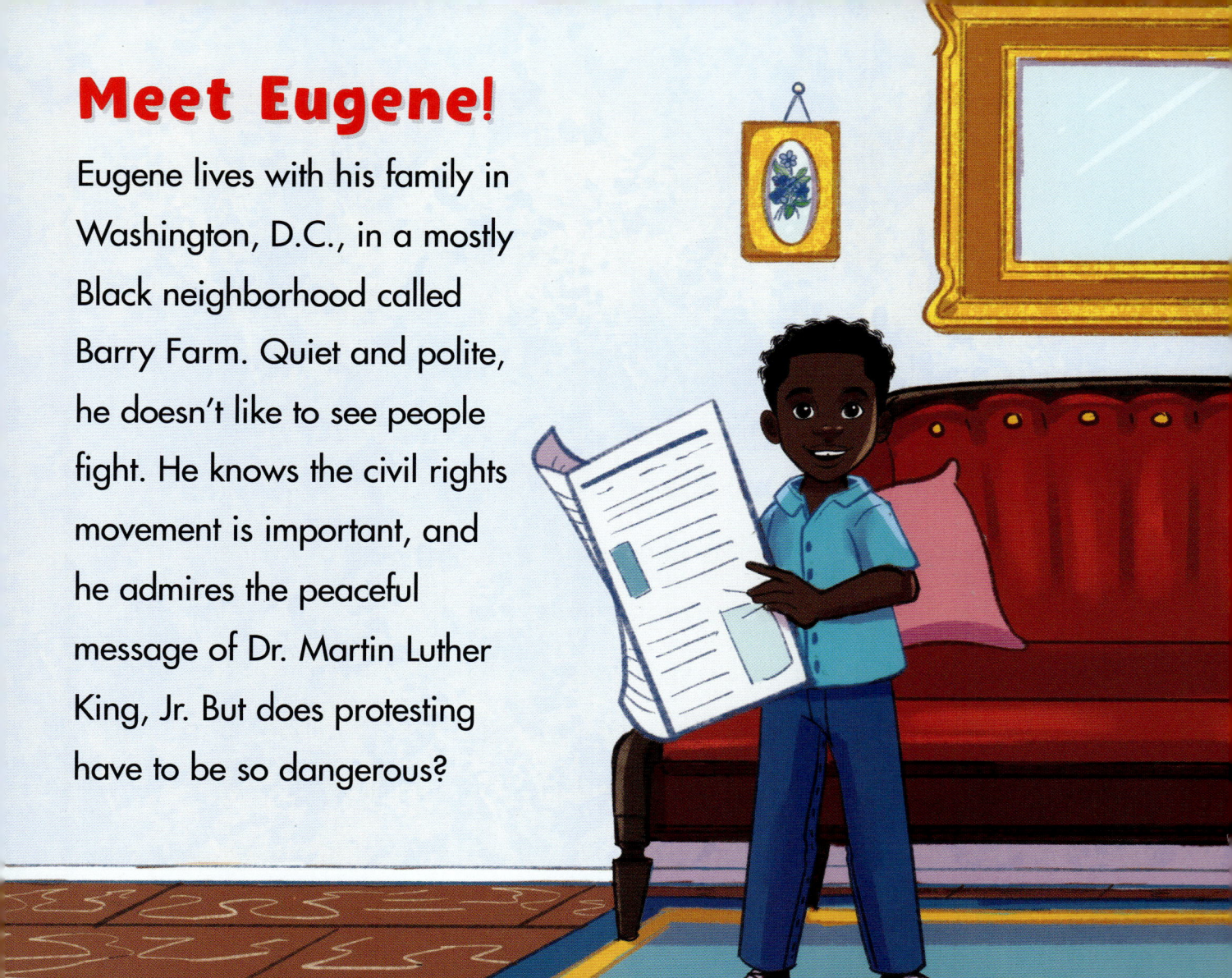

Meet Lori!

Lori is Eugene's little sister. She loves to play outside and read comic books. She knows that her family isn't always treated fairly. But to her, protests and laws seem like things for adults to worry about. She would rather focus on having fun and enjoying her summer break . . .

Eugene sighed as he set down the newspaper. He was happy to read about people fighting for equal rights. But he wasn't happy at all to see angry people using violence to fight back against the protestors.

Dad set his hand on Eugene's shoulder. "People are doing great work with these protests," he said. "I think it's time for me to join in."

Eugene swallowed hard. What if Dad got hurt? Or arrested?

DON'T FIGHT BACK

Black people faced a lot of racist violence in 1963. But many civil rights leaders insisted that people should not use violence to fight back against racists. Instead, by remaining peaceful, they would show people how cruel the racists were. This was called **nonviolent civil disobedience**.

Nonviolent civil disobedience was inspired by Mahatma Gandhi. He helped free the country of India from British colonial rule without using violence.

Later that night, the whole family was watching TV. A news report said that Dr. Martin Luther King, Jr., had been arrested for leading a protest march.

"Now, that's a leader," Mom said. Dad and Eugene nodded in agreement.

Lori didn't see what was so special about Dr. King. He reminded her of the preacher at church. "Can we change the channel?" she asked. "I want to watch something fun."

TUNING IN TO THE REVOLUTION

By the late 1950s, most Americans had televisions in their homes for the first time. They could see for themselves how poorly Black people were being treated. On news reports, they saw people get sprayed by water hoses and beaten by police, or jailed just for protesting. People also got to see how great a speaker Dr. King was.

At a civil rights protest on May 3, 1963, in Birmingham, Alabama, police used dogs to attack peaceful marchers. Many of the marchers were children.

11

A few weeks later, Dad had big news. "There's going to be a protest march right here in Washington," he said. "And we're all going."

"Won't it be dangerous?" Eugene asked.

"Don't worry," Dad said. "I've signed up as a marshal. I'll help keep the peace."

Dad's words didn't make Eugene feel much better. Lori wasn't happy, either.

"It's going to be hot," she complained. "And speeches are boring. Can't I stay home?"

"Absolutely not," Mom said. "This is important."

WE GOT YOUR BACK!

Marshals were volunteers who helped keep everyone safe and healthy at the march. They wore white caps and gold bands on their arms. They gave directions and helped stop any fights. They also made sure people did not faint from the heat—it was a hot day that almost reached 85 degrees!

Two marshals get ready to assist members of the crowd during the March on Washington.

Mom and Dad worked hard to help prepare for the march. They went to meetings. They handed out instructions for the march to other people in town. Eugene and Lori helped them make signs for people to carry. They both started to feel more excited about the march.

Then, one night, Eugene heard Mom and Dad whispering. He thought he heard Dad say something about a bomb threat. He got a tight feeling in his stomach. Would the march be dangerous after all?

MAKING PLANS

The march was officially called the March on Washington for Jobs and Freedom. The planning was led by activists Bayard Rustin and A. Philip Randolph. They built a network of volunteers across the country. Thousands of people—women and men—helped raise funds, create signs, and even pack more than 80,000 lunches to hand out. In a time before the internet, all of this had to be organized over the phone, through the mail, or in person.

Bayard Rustin (left) and A. Philip Randolph (right) had decades of experience as organizers.

Finally, the big day arrived. Dad tied a golden band around his arm and put a white cap on his head to show he was a marshal. Mom carried a stack of booklets labeled "Organizing Manual." As they arrived at the Washington Monument, Eugene handed Lori a sign to hold.

"Where are all the people?" she asked.

Eugene looked around. The crowd was sparse.

"Don't worry," Dad said. "We're just getting started."

He and Mom exchanged smiles.

ALL ABOARD!

It took a lot of effort to get people to the march. The organizers wanted as many people as possible to attend. But they knew not everyone could afford to pay for their own travel. Volunteers helped arrange bus rides for people. This allowed marchers to come from distant cities like Birmingham, Alabama, and St. Louis, Missouri. Some people also came by car, train, and airplane.

Residents of Nashville, Tennessee, gather at a local church to board a bus to Washington for the march.

Soon, busloads of people began arriving. The crowd grew and grew.

"Wow," Eugene said. "You weren't kidding, Dad!"

"It's like an ocean of people!" Lori added.

They all began marching together toward the Lincoln Memorial. People sang, chanted, and held their signs high. Lori was surprised that it wasn't boring at all. She felt a special kind of excitement in her chest. It wasn't like anything she'd ever felt before.

A CROWD LIKE NO OTHER

Organizers were afraid the march would have low attendance. It was held on a Wednesday because many people went to church on the weekends and many church organizations helped plan the march. But more than 250,000 people showed up to the March on Washington—far more than expected.

The crowd occupied the entire National Mall.

Eugene felt excited, too. But as he marched, he kept a close eye out for signs of danger. There were lots of police and soldiers around, but they didn't make him feel safe. He knew they were often the ones fighting back against protestors.

As he marched, Eugene noticed a man walking toward him. The man was carrying a black bag. The words *bomb threat* flashed across Eugene's mind.

STAYING SAFE

Being safe was a big worry at the march. At other civil rights protests, racist people had made violent attacks on peaceful protestors. Thousands of police officers were at the march. But sadly, some organizers believed that the police might not be there to protect Black people. At previous protests, police had attacked and arrested protesters instead of protecting them. Despite the fears, the march was peaceful. There were no violent incidents reported.

Around 5,900 Washington, D.C., police officers and 6,000 National Guardsmen and soldiers helped keep the peace at the march.

Eugene gulped as the man drew near. What should he do?

Suddenly, the man smiled. He unzipped the bag and pulled out a cloth bundle.

"Mind helping me?" he asked Eugene. "This is a two-person job." He handed part of the cloth to Eugene, then unrolled the rest. It was a banner.

Eugene sighed in relief. He held the banner proudly alongside his new friend as they continued marching.

SIGNS OF PROTEST

The march's organizers did not want everyone to carry their own homemade signs. Instead, premade signs were provided by groups such as churches and employee organizations. People of all races from diverse backgrounds holding the same signs was an important signal of **solidarity**. However, some people brought their own signs anyway.

Different organizations created their own signs for their members to carry at the march.

Eventually, the marching crowd arrived at the Lincoln Memorial. Everyone listened carefully as speakers took turns delivering inspiring messages from a stage near the memorial. Finally, it was time to hear from Dr. King.

Lori listened carefully. She realized that her mom had been right: He was a great leader.

"I can't see," she said, tugging on Dad's sleeve.

He smiled and set Lori on his shoulders.

She watched and listened, smiling the whole time.

"I HAVE A DREAM"

Many civil rights leaders spoke at the march. But the one who made the biggest impact was Dr. Martin Luther King, Jr. In the best-known part of his historic speech, King spoke of his dream that children of all races would one day be able to play together. But this wasn't a planned part of his speech. As King spoke, a singer named Mahalia Jackson yelled, "Tell 'em about the dream, Martin!" This inspired King to set aside his notes and **improvise** his most famous words.

Civil rights activist Daisy Bates was the only woman allowed to give a speech at the march.

"What an amazing turnout," Mom said as they walked home.

"It won't solve all our problems," Dad said. "But this was an important day."

"'I have a dream,'" Lori said, imitating Dr. King. She knew she would remember his speech for the rest of her life.

"When's the next protest?" Eugene asked. He wasn't afraid anymore. There was work to do. And he was ready to help.

THE NEXT STEPS

The March on Washington had a major impact on the civil rights movement. A year later, the new president, Lyndon B. Johnson, signed the Civil Rights Act of 1964. This law banned racial discrimination and guaranteed voting rights for people of color. It also banned segregation in schools and jobs. It was not the end of the civil rights movement, however. Even today, Black people and other minority groups continue to fight for equality in America.

Dr. King and other people watch as President Lyndon B. Johnson (seated) signs the Civil Rights Act of 1964 into law.

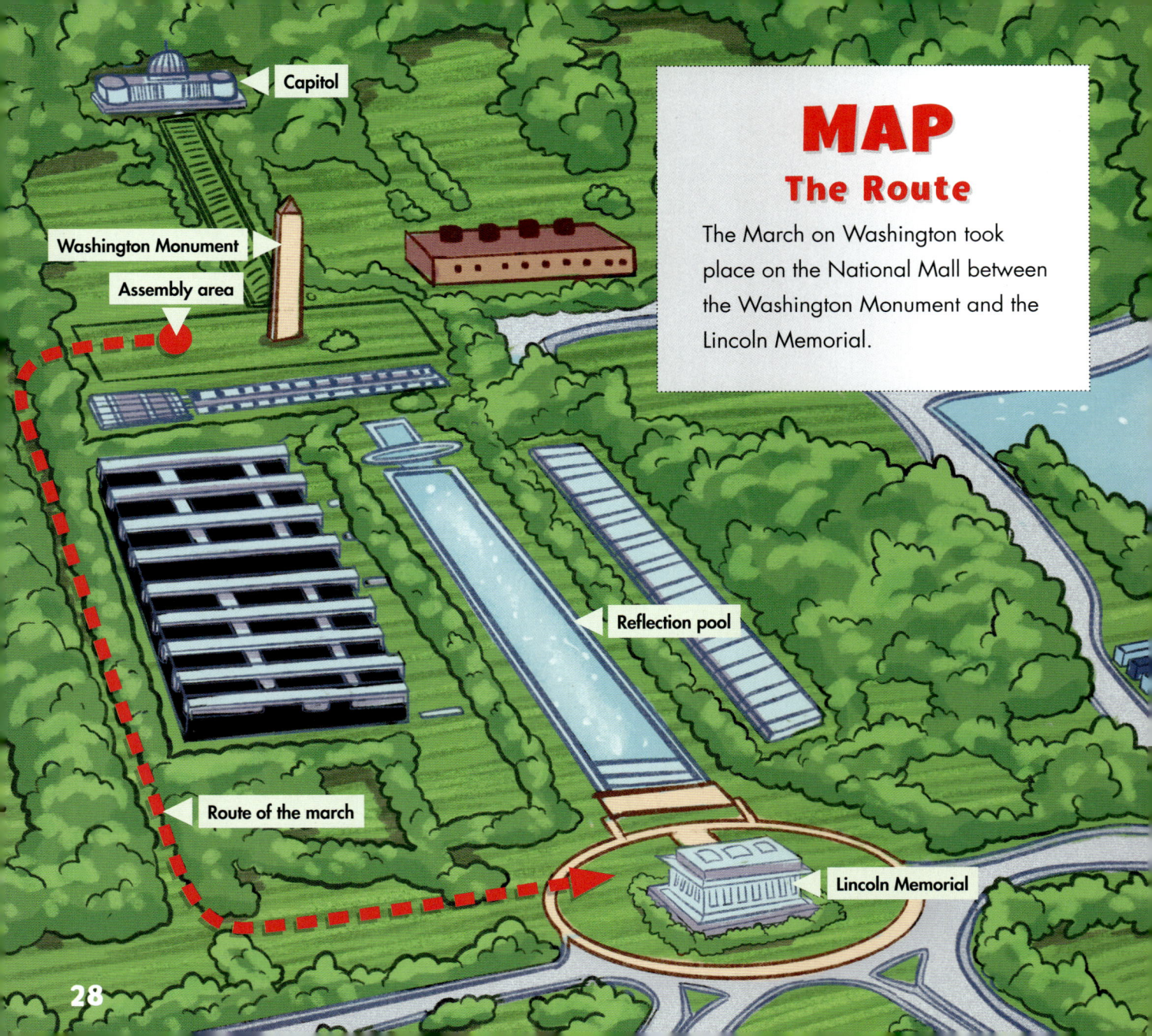

Capitol

Washington Monument

Assembly area

MAP
The Route

The March on Washington took place on the National Mall between the Washington Monument and the Lincoln Memorial.

Reflection pool

Route of the march

Lincoln Memorial

TIMELINE

1941 A. Philip Randolph plans a march on Washington but cancels it after President Franklin D. Roosevelt issues an executive order to create a committee to prevent job discrimination. It is called the Fair Employment Practice Committee (FEPC).

1946 Congress votes to eliminate the FEPC, upsetting civil rights activists.

1957 A. Philip Randolph and Bayard Rustin begin working together with Dr. Martin Luther King, Jr., to organize protest events around the country. Together, they hold the Prayer Pilgrimage for Freedom in Washington, D.C., drawing about 25,000 attendees.

1963 Over 250,000 people attend the March on Washington for Jobs and Freedom and hear Dr. King's famous "I Have a Dream" speech.

1964 The success of the March on Washington leads President Lyndon B. Johnson to push Congress into passing the Civil Rights Act of 1964. This bans segregation in public places such as restaurants and hotels and guarantees voting rights for people of color.

1965 Congress passes the Voting Rights Act, prohibiting racial discrimination in voting.

Today People across America continue to fight for equality and civil rights.

WORDS TO KNOW

civil rights (SIV-uhl RITES) the individual rights that all members of a democratic society have to freedom and equal treatment under the law

colonial (kuh-LOH-nee-uhl) relating to a territory that has been settled by people from another country and is controlled by that country

improvise (IM-pruh-vize) to make something up on short notice

Indigenous (in-DI-juh-nuhs) of or relating to the earliest known inhabitants of a place and especially of a place that was colonized

Jim Crow laws (JIM KROW LAWZ) laws passed to enforce racial segregation after slavery was banned

nonviolent civil disobedience (nahn-VYE-uh-luhnt SIV-uhl dis-uh-BEE-dee-uhns) the practice of peacefully disobeying laws as a form of protest

segregation (seg-ri-GAY-shuhn) the act or practice of keeping people or groups apart

sit-ins (SIT-inz) protest events in which Black people peacefully occupied segregated, whites-only public places, such as restaurants

solidarity (sah-lih-DARE-ih-tee) a show of strength in togetherness

INDEX

ABOUT THE AUTHORS

Josh Gregory is the author of more than 250 books for young readers, covering everything from U.S. history to technology and video games. He is from Chicago, Illinois.

Aaron Talley is a teacher and writer who lives in Chicago, Illinois. He loves to inspire his students and all kids everywhere to follow their passions! He is originally from Detroit, Michigan.

ABOUT THE ILLUSTRATOR

Ana Latese is an African-American illustrator and character designer who enjoys producing beautiful imagery inspired by vibrant colors, fantasy elements, and joy. Ana has worked with clients such as the *Washington Post*, Penguin Random House, Hulu, and Scholastic. When she's not illustrating, she loves to play video games, drink a nice cup of tea at a cafe, or binge-watch TV series.